White Sore Rump

Recounted by W. F. Goose

Written by P. J. Taylor

Based on an original idea by Jenny Campbell.

Cheers, Jen.

White Front Sore Rump

Copyright © 2014 Philip James Taylor

All rights reserved.

ISBN-13: 9781495999291

ISBN-10: 1495999297

This book is a work of fiction. The characters, locations, and incidents portrayed are products of the author's imagination, or used fictitiously. Any resemblance to actual events, places, or persons, living or dead, is entirely a coincidence.

Visit www.blackerminetales.co.uk for more stories by the author.

ONE

I was kissing the sky ... and it slapped me in the rump. BANG! – followed by *pifft pifft pifft*, three of my primary feathers ripped away.

Oi! Come back! They were good primaries, solid – the kind that'd do a round trip to the Arctic. I glanced back to inspect the damage. My right wing had gone. I looked up. The sky had gone too, but something – *the Sun?* – was burning right through my rump.

Left wing flailing, I span and twisted through a brown, green, and red blur.

Red? What in Whooper's name is Red???

Oi! I caught sight of my lost primaries plummeting down – or up? – I wasn't sure which. The ground had been replaced by a blue sheet with fluffy white things, while the sky had become this murky brown mass that rushed towards me in a way that the sky really shouldn't – SMACK!

I'd hit the ground. At least that's what I'd thought, until I started to sink.

Slimy weed wrapped around my neck and pulled me down into darkness; I thrashed and pecked and wrenched. Fish and beetley things darted away in the gloom, and two dangerous eyes watched patiently, waiting for me to die … and then:

Ahhhhhh, sweet air. I bobbed on the surface, remembering that I could float.

I paddled to the bank, because one wing was exhausted and the other had gone. Ok, not gone, as it turned out, just at a weird angle. The Sun continued to burn right through my rump – from underwater! Didn't think it could do that. Sneaky devil.

I slopped onto the muddy bank and inspected the damage: a few feathers gone, nothing that wouldn't grow back, and a backside peppered with black holes leaking hot, red liquid. I jabbed my beak down one, for good measure…

WHOAH!!! Whiteout – and a screeching, tortured honk – one that gave me *mouse pimples*. I glanced around for the goose making such a bloodcurdling shriek, but the rest of the flock stared back at me.

Ahhh, right, gotcha. I stopped screeching.

"Sorry," I muttered, as Uncle Joe swam over to join me. He lowered his long neck and eyed up my wings and leaky rump.

"Well," he concluded, "that's the end of you."

And that was the day I died.

TWO

Honk, Honk, HONK, SPLASH ... quiet bubbling ... then frantic swishing and a small crash as I broke the surface and floated.

That was the end of my many attempts to re-kiss the sky – so I'm not dead, *technically* – just dead in terms of being a goose.

"I told you so," said Uncle Joe, "What did I say?"

I didn't look at him. Instead, I hung my head and stared at the scrawny White-fronted Goose peering up at me from the surface of the water.

What's that scrawny goose's problem? Always following me around until I peck at him, and then BAM – Mr Upside-down is gone.

I answered Uncle Joe, "You said I'd never –"

"– never fly again," he finished, as if I wasn't there. "And I was right. And it's your own fault. What did I say about flying over a NUB who's crouched in the reeds?"

"You said they'd be out to –"

"– out to get you. And I was right."

NUBs, or 'Naked Upright Badgers', are those weird mammals that strut around on their hind legs as if they own the place – and who cover themselves in wool from the backs of sheep.

"But," I said, "NUBs at this end of the marsh – they're nice – the ones who shelter in those big nests made of sliced trees."

Uncle Joe gave a honk of disdain, "Mammals. What do I say about mammals?"

"That you can't –"

"– can't trust them. Not one. Not so much as a Water Vole. Remember this egg of wisdom, it'll save your life one day."

Wisdom dispensed, he swam away, beak held high.

Hmmm. I need a distraction from being grounded. The flock will provide, always does. Ah, here we go...

"Hello Mr White, Mrs White," I nodded respectfully at the pair of geese drifting past, "how's life? Do you fancy a swim past the NUB nests – see if we can't make those lightning flashes appear?"

"Goodness me no," said Mr White.

"No time for superfluous swimming," said Mrs White.

"Or other such frivolities," added Mr White.

"It's time for eating: vegetation, vegetation, vegetation," said Mrs White ... or maybe Mr White.

"Delicious and nutritious..." and I gave up telling them apart. "Build up those fat reserves..." *"Nearly breeding season."* "I thought maybe ... a second brood this year, nudge nudge..." *"Darling! Not in front of the neighbours."* "Oh, young Whitey here doesn't mind, strapping young goose like him, mind's not on anything else, eh?"

A pause. Both Mr and Mrs White stared at me.

"Err…" I realised I should say something, "…actually, I'm not going on migration."

The two-headed goose of Mr and Mrs White paused, looked at each other, then back at me, and honked with laughter.

"Hiiilaaarious!" said Mr White.

"You are such a joker," said Mrs White.

"No … seriously. Me and Uncle Joe are going to stay here for summer, cruise around, eat some veg…"

"Really?" said Mr White, "Are you certain? I heard that Old Joe's leading the V – leading the first leg of migration."

"What?! He's leaving without me?"

"Oh yes," Mrs White nodded, "Call of the tundra, and what have you. He's ever so proud."

I was already swimming away.

"Don't rush," called Mr and / or Mrs White, "you'll waste valuable fat reserves: essential for the long flight ahead..."

Uncle Joe was already flexing his wings when I found him bobbing on the water.

"But..." I pleaded, "...you can't just leave me. What will I do here?"

"Stupid things, no doubt, just like your parents. What did I say to them?"

The Sun began to burn again, but not from above, and not on my holey backside – but from somewhere deep in my breast. It was hot. A hiss escaped my beak:

"Don't speak about my p–"

"– I said not to fly through that meadow of giant white flowers – those rotating petals will knock you right out of the sky. And what did they do?"

I didn't need his answer: I knew. I would always know. But Uncle Joe's words narrated the images in my head: redness and feathers and falling...

"Right through the middle, slap, bang, quicker than a falcon. No, they should've listened to Old Joe. Anyway, what's done is done. I've got to go – leading the V this year – an honour, a great honour."

"But..."

"Sorry, young Whitey, the tundra's calling – all that *slightly* green land out there, crying for our return – can't you hear it?" He started flapping.

"Yes, of course. Of course I can hear it..."

But I heard other sounds that were more obvious – like the storm of heavy wing beats, and water swishing around webbed feet. The flock – a huge twisting, twirling creature – peeled off the marsh, honking and beating its way into the sky.

"Of course I can hear it…" but my own honking was lost amongst the others.

Higher and higher they soared.

"It's saying: No hurry, plenty of time, don't leave poor Whitey behind…"

The flock entered the V formation.

"…can't migrate without Whitey. It's saying… Oh, who am I kidding? I don't know what it's saying. We're not on speaking terms."

I looked down at the calm water and saw that scrawny goose again: Mr Upside-down. He looked sad. Maybe if he didn't disappear with every splash, he could be my friend. If I just … aw, nope. I'd moved my feet and he'd vanished, replaced by ripples.

And that was the day I became the only White-front on the marsh.

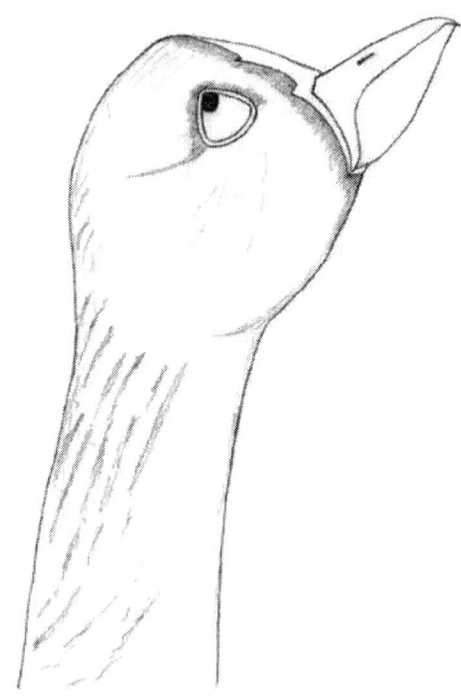

THREE

After the flock left, winter seemed to follow them – everything going North without me, even the weather.

Well ... fine, I thought, *I don't need them, I'm a survivor (probably). This goose is going solo. This goose is heading for some lunch.*

And yet ... no flock. That was weird. That made me a bit shivery. There'd always been the flock...

Feeding: in the flock.

Roosting: in the flock.

Flying: in the flock.

I'd been part of it, part of something special ... and suddenly ... a flock of one?

Not really a flock – not even a goose – can't have a goose without the flock. How could I feed, without those many eyes keeping watch?

No, can't feed, can't roost, can't fly. I'm not a goose: I'm falcon food.

Pull yourself together. Goose up.

It was feeding time, and so, one webbed foot after another, I padded over to the field of sugar beet – *mmmmm scrummy* – and chowed down until I heard … *humming?*

A shadow raced across the ground – a hawk, a falcon, a demon – *but humming?*

Ahhh, gotcha!

Nonchalant, I carried on eating as the humming whirled above my head.

"Morning Snipe," I said to thin air.

"Snipe?" said an indignant voice, "Snipe?! There's no Snipe here. You're mistaken, completely mistaken: wrong, incorrect, false."

"I can hear you humming above me."

"It's called *drumming* … and no, that sound isn't above – it's everywhere, emanating from deep within the earth – a primal tone that crosses the eons from the dawn of time…"

"Have you got a girlfriend yet?"

A raspy bark sounded from above and Snipe landed in front of me. He was a plump bird with a long, thin beak – a beak that clearly belonged on a much bigger, leaner bird. The humming had stopped.

"No," Snipe shook his head, twiggy beak swishing through the air. "Don't be ridiculous, there's no lady snipe for miles around: nothing, zero, zilch."

"Then why are you wasting your time?"

"Wasting? Not wasted. Got to keep at it, keep with the program: the call of the wild. Keep the tail feathers spruced, keep the air rushing through to create 'The Drumming' – such music, such beauty – poetry of the wind." He stared into space for a moment, then looked sharply at me, "and what is it that geese do … in matters of love?"

"Errrrr…" I said, and it was a long errrr, longer than any errrr before, "…honk. I think."

"Then honk. Honk your heart out, honk at the wind itself – honk at the sky and at the mountains – ascend to a level of honking never before seen in all of goosekind – and so when your lady goose arrives, she is overcome by perfection…"

"Right," I said, because I wasn't sure what other words I could slot into that awkward silence – not without indicating he was a bit soft in the head. "Not sure that'll happen. All the lady geese went North without me. All the ganders too. In fact, every goose of every species. It's just me now."

"Then it seems you are one of a kind: alone, solitary, unique. But fear not! Honk at the wind … and your day will come. You have my word."

"Right … and how long have you been honking – I mean, *drumming* – at the wind?"

"Ten summers."

"Ten! But that's … one, two…" I lost count, so started again, "one, two…" Nope – this counting business was tricky, "…that's longer than I've been alive…"

No … honking at the wind seemed like a bad idea all round. What I needed, was a second opinion – and I knew where I could get one, because I could hear something on the wind – and it wasn't honking or drumming … it sounded more like: PeeeeeeeeeeeeeWIT!

"Thanks, Snipe." I dipped my beak, respectfully, "Thanks for your advice – which in no way sounds like a waste of time." I waddled off.

And that was the day I went for a second opinion.

FOUR

"PeeeeeWITT!"

A black and white blur zigzagged across the sky.

What in Whooper's name is wrong with these birds?

"PeeeeeWITT!"

Ouch! That crazy alarm call sliced into my head.

Lapwing ... I knew there was a reason I'd never honked with them before: migraines.

"PeeeeeWITT!" A twist and dive; black and white; role then plummet; veer left, veer right and ... "PeeeeeWITT!"

"Excuse me," I shouted over the screeches bouncing around my ear holes. I heard a whoop of air and a big flappy thing dropped out of the sky. But the wings were quickly folded away to reveal a dapper bird: white chest, dark glossy back, wings and tail glimmering purple, green and black. A slender crest on the top of its head waved in the breeze.

"Good day to you, young goose," the Lapwing stepped forward. "Squadron Leader L.W. Ing, Green Plover Flight, at your service," he bobbed, then glanced over his shoulder. "Stand down the alarm: the raid is over…" and from the rushes stumbled three little balls of speckled fluff, all with tiny beaks and legs and eyes.

"All present and correct," the Lapwing bobbed with pride. "Capital, capital!"

"Errr … if I'm interrupting, I can come back…"

"Nonsense, not at all, just following procedure. Lieutenant Vanellus: status report…"

A swoop and a whoosh. Another Lapwing tumbled from the sky, her markings less distinct than the Squadron Leader.

"Mummy, mummy, mummy…" the balls of fluff tumbled towards the newcomer.

"Halt!" snapped the Squadron Leader. "Aaaatenshun!"

The fluffy balls rolled to a stop.

"Discipline, children, discipline. Flight Lieutenant Mummy – I mean, Flight Lieutenant *Vanellus* – is about to make a report. Continue, Flight Lieutenant…"

"Heavy losses," Vanellus bowed her head. "Three broods gone from the large marsh, two from the lower mire."

The Squadron Leader shook his head. "Truly, this is our darkest hour. You are relieved, Flight Lieutenant. Attend to your domestic duties." She walked away, the three chicks scampering between her legs. "Now," the Squadron Leader turned back to me, "What can I do for you, Sir?"

Good question. Fix my wing. Carry me to the tundra.

"I'm sort of at a loss. My flock migrated without me."

"Last goose standing, eh? Behind enemy lines: trapped and desperate. We've all been there: backs to the rushes – white leg moments, I call them."

"Well … I'm not sure it's as dramatic as –"

" – And you're lacking purpose, eh? Survivor's guilt, maybe? Want to sign up and do your duty. That's the spirit!" He examined me carefully, "You're a bit … plumper, than my usual recruits. Ever engaged a squadron of crows?"

"Not really."

"Ah, heavy bomber then. What's your aim like?"

"My aim?"

"Yes – your aim," he pointed a wing at my rump, "the guano, lad, the guano: aerial bombardment."

"I've honestly never tried."

"What about running interference?"

"Interference?"

"Swearing, lad, swearing – puts Old Corvy right off. I don't like to use such bad language in front of the chicks, but desperate times … give it a go…"

"Errr…"

"The P-word, lad, the P-word."

"Erm … Peewit?"

"Rubbish. Won't frighten so much as a pipit. Sorry, lad, you're just not cut out for military service. Now, better take cover, I see dark shapes approaching…"

Raucous calls filled the air as big, black birds rowed solidly towards us.

"Cawwwww," said a crow, "Cawww blimey, look at those little chicks. Cawwwww, they look tasty."

"Get all fighting birds off the ground!" bellowed the Squadron Leader, and from a seemingly empty field of rushes, Lapwing rose up, big flappy wings beating down as they ascended.

"Let them have it lads, let the *peeewits* have it!"

"PEEEEEEEEE WITT!"

"CAWWWWW – ouch! Cawww blimey, that hurt..."

I watched the battle – twisting black and white versus solid black ... and then I watched a single crow walk unnoticed along the ground ... towards the clump of rushes where the fluffy chicks sheltered.

I stepped forwards, but a voice from behind said:

"Cawwwww blimey, I'd get out of here ... if you know what's good for you."

And that was the day, when – despite NOT knowing what's good for me – I did get out of there – as fast as I could waddle. I wish I hadn't.

The crows are coming...

Will you fight?

FIVE

There was only one type of animal left on the marsh to talk to – and I was *not* keen – not keen at all. It took many sunrises and sunsets to pluck up the courage.

They – and there were plenty of them to go around – were *Feral* geese. Long ago, so the legend says, they'd been Greylags, migrating in vast scraggly Vs to the tundra and back – not neat and tidy like those prissy Pink-feet, all style and no substance – but honest, hardworking geese. Eat, mate, fledge, repeat – forever.

Except one day ... they'd given it all up and become degenerate monsters ... so the legend says – or at least, my Uncle Joe. *"Don't speak to the feral geese. Don't go near them. Don't so much as ruffle a feather in their direction."*

But looking at them, they didn't seem quite so monstrous or degenerate, with their drab brown plumage and carroty orange beaks – but I could see two reasons why White-fronts might be scared:

1. They were a little bigger than us.

2. There were more of them – much more, now I was waddling solo.

But they were eating grass like the best of us, so I held my beak high and paddled over to the nearest pair.

"Hello," I said.

"Hey goose," one of the Greylags replied. "How's it goin'?"

"Not so good. I've got a wing out of action and my flock migrated without me."

"Aw, that's harsh, goose, that's ice cold…" The Greylag glanced over his shoulder at his female companion, who nodded, "…but think of it as an opportunity … the chance of a better life."

"So it's not a problem being…"

"…bein' what?" I had the male Greylag's full attention.

"You know…" I leaned closer, "…*feral*."

The female goose swam forwards and laughed, "Feral! You poor naïve gosling. Feral is a term for dogs foaming at the mouth. We're not feral, we're … naturalised … sedentary … on a different evolutionary path. My gander describes it best," she jabbed her beak in his breast, "what do you always say?"

"That we're on *Easy Marsh*," said the male Greylag.

"There you go: *Easy Marsh*. Now," she jabbed him again, "you tell the poor little gosling all about the joys of *Easy Marsh*; I'm going for my morning swim."

"Sure thing, hen, you take care, missin' you already… Now, where to begin? *Easy Marsh*," He placed a wing gently over my nape, keeping one eye on the female goose drifting on the silver water, "There ain't no migration; no chuffin' and puffin' across frozen seas," his gaze followed her, "all you can eat, everyday: grass, roots ... and a whole field of beets." The female goose disappeared behind some reeds. The Greylag's wing clamped around me, pulling my neck so that it was barely a beak's length from his own, "Get out, goose."

"What?"

"Get out while you can."

"I don't understand…"

"If you can't fly, goose, then paddle, swim, waddle – just get away from here and don't come back."

"But you said –"

"– Never mind what I said – all just fog and mist – to keep my hen happy – no need to worry her pretty little head about it. She's sharp, but she don't see it – she's too close."

"See what?"

"That we're trapped. Stay a summer – that's how it started – just one – we can go anytime – we can feel the lines of the earth, always. But it's been too long, goose, too many generations. I can't feel 'em, those invisible lines, pointin' North – can't feel a thing. We can never migrate again. Ever."

"But if it's so easy here…"

"Take those fields of beets … they're also full of bangs: BANG, BANG, BANG – so we fly away, but nothin' happens – so we go back and eat. But sometimes ... sometimes after one of those bangs, a goose can fall from the sky and not get up." He looked around, as if expecting one to drop at any moment. "It's the NUBs, goose – they don't like us – because we don't do what real geese should. Last season, a NUB walked around the marsh, around all the nests – and what happened? No hatches. Not one. Bad year, bad luck – but *listen*, goose," he brought his head even closer, "I seen 'em – the NUBs – I seen 'em pierce those eggs with somethin' sharper than a Curlew's beak. Then they're dead."

"But ... why?"

"Like I said, we don't do what we should. You know the name of an animal that don't do what it should?"

I shook my head.

"*Carrion*. Now, you start waddlin' fast and – ahhh, hey hen, lookin' good!" The female goose stepped out of the water; the male loosened his wing-hold of me. "Now then ... our goose here, he's just goin' – I've given him the low down on *Easy Marsh*, I have. He knows what to do – ain't that right goose?"

I nodded.

"At a goose! Now scram..."

And that was the day I left the marsh forever.

SIX

Slam! A freezing wave hit me. SLAM – again – despite the sun shining – despite me standing on dry land miles from the sea.

SLAM! Solid impact sent a quivering shock down my back, exploding off every feather – off every barbule in my body: this was fear – and it burnt me with ice.

Okay. It's okay, I repeated this thought again and again until I tricked myself – *slightly* – into believing it.

The heavy fear settled in my breast. I felt stuck to the spot, but at least I could think ... and I tried not to think it was the end of everything ... because I couldn't feel them ... the invisible travel lines ... the tingling buzz running through the rocks of the earth, converging on the poles, on the tundra, showing the way to migrate. They'd gone. I didn't know which way to go.

I looked at my peppered rump. Surely I can't have sensed them using my rump? Nothing important is in the rump – well – nothing important for navigation.

They'll come back…

But it had been many sunrises and sunsets since I was shot.

Have they been gone all this time?

Gone.

The End.

Of everything.

Of me.

And something was whistling and humming at the same time – a whistley hum or a hummy whistle – like the wind over rocks, and it came from a pink splodge in a tree. A bird?

Okay. It's okay. Not only will I migrate while grounded – I'll do it by asking for directions. No shame in that. No shame at all.

I waddled over to the tree.

"Hello there," I said to the pink splodge.

The whistley hum faded. A plump bird hopped onto a low branch that bent under its weight.

"Oh hello, Sir, hello. Such a good day, don't you think?" the pink splodge raised a chunky beak to the sky, "But there's a storm brewing, Sir, a terrible storm, mark my whistley hums – blow away the marsh, it will, that's the truth, Sir, the honest truth. The Buzzard told me so."

"Errr … yes," I looked up at clear blue skies and blinding sun. "Who are you, by the way?"

The bird puffed up his podgy chest to become almost spherical, his black cap, beady eyes, and thick beak almost lost in the ball of pinkness. "Bullfinch," it said proudly, "Bullfinch by name, Bullfinch by nature. How may I be of service?"

"Have you seen a flock of White-fronted Geese fly over?"

"Of course, Sir, of course – and such a flock you never did see! The sky turned dark – night time, I thought to myself, night time come early – a conspiracy by the foxes, no doubt."

"Right ... and which way was this flock heading?"

"To the hills…" he held out one wing, "…and to the vast ocean beyond…"

"Ocean beyond the hills?" Uncle Joe had never mentioned that.

"Oh yes, Sir – a purple ocean of boiling water – fish that leap out and swallow you whole – the injustice, Sir, the travesty of mere *fish* eating a bird – a piscatorial nightmare of *Pandian* proportions. Shakes me to my porous bones, it does."

"Yes, I'm sure it does. These White-fronts … can you describe them?"

"Of course, Sir. Vast birds – huge – their entire head the purest white, blinding in its majesty. A light to rival the sun itself."

"A blinding light … that somehow made the sky go dark?"

"Of course. Well … dark at first … then light, as my eyes adjusted. Oh the light, Sir, dazzling it was – dazzling!" His wings fluttered with enthusiasm but did nothing to lift his bulk.

"Hmm. I see. And what type of goose do you think I am?"

"The finest, Sir, the mightiest…"

"But what species?"

"Well…" Bullfinch ruffled the feathers of his bulging breast, "…that is to say … I'm not quite sure, Sir … but there are echoes of The Great Goose in you, the Ruby Crested Goose, and not to mention the Giant Bear-eating Goose of –"

"I'm a White-front."

"Oh."

"Not quite like the White-fronts you saw in the sky, am I?"

"Well … not as such, Sir, not as such … but then the sun was so strong, Sir, blinding…"

"The sun reflecting off their white heads?"

"Oh yes, Sir, glaring it was."

"The white heads that they *didn't* have – that also made the sky go dark?"

"Precisely, Sir, precisely." A pause. "No ... wait. Well ... not quite all-white heads, Sir, maybe a hint of brown, maybe a –"

"Bullfinch," I cut him off, "thanks for your help, but I think I'll find my own way."

"Of course, Sir, a pleasure conversing with you, mind how you go."

And that was the day I decided never to ask Bullfinch for directions ever again.

SEVEN

Invisible lines or no invisible lines – I simply needed to find the sea and turn right – and that would point me towards the tundra. Then it would simply be a case of bypassing the land of ice – and reaching the *slightly* green land beyond. Easy.

The trouble was, I hadn't lived on a marsh by the coast. *My* marsh had been beside an inland loch. Simply finding the actual sea would be tricky.

I set out waddling towards Bullfinch's hills – not because I expected some purple ocean on the other side, but because I needed a vantage point. And they were big hills. I knew this because, even after many sunrises and sunsets, they hadn't got any closer.

I swam up streams and brooks, roosted in reed beds, and waddled through sheep fields. The snooty occupants kept themselves to themselves...

"Baaaah," one ewe laughed, when I asked her where the tundra was. "Baaaah, good luck with that..." she walked back to her lambs, shaking her head. She'd be *baaahing* on the other side of her face when a NUB stole her fleece.

I started talking to myself, "Keep going, Whitey." *"Let's stop for food, Whitey."* "Good idea, Whitey, you're such a clever goose." *"Oh stop it, Whitey!"* "No, you stop it..." then eventually, I talked to trees, rocks, and the sky...

"Please provide some shade."

"Get out of the way, you igneous fool!"

"Please cloud over, it's SOOOOO hot."

I thought maybe I was going crazy ... and one day, when the grass talked back, I knew it was true...

"Steady!" said a tussock. "Nearly there, bear with me, bear with me."

I sat down, ready to 'bear with' the meadow grass wafting in the breeze. A squat, black beetle lumbered out of the tussock, "Onwards, tally ho!" and then – BUMP – it walked straight into me. The beetle stopped, flexed its antennae, backed up a few steps … then walked forwards again: BUMP.

"Hello there," I called down.

"Oh…" The beetle rose up on its front legs, "…didn't see you there. I was just about to –"

And a chorus of tiny voices shouted, *"Dung! Dung! Dung!"* They seemed to come from inside the beetle itself.

"Quiet!" snapped the beetle, turning slowly around on the spot, "Hush now; settle down. I'll have order. I *will* have order." It completed its turn and peered up at me. "Sorry about that – it's my mites, you see – little devils tend to get impatient when they're hungry."

"Dung! Dung! Dung!"

"Yes, quite … settle down. Now, allow me to introduce myself … Mr Dor, Dung Beetle Extraordinaire, at your service, ready and waiting…" There was a long pause; Mr Dor's antennae twitched. "Now then … where were we?"

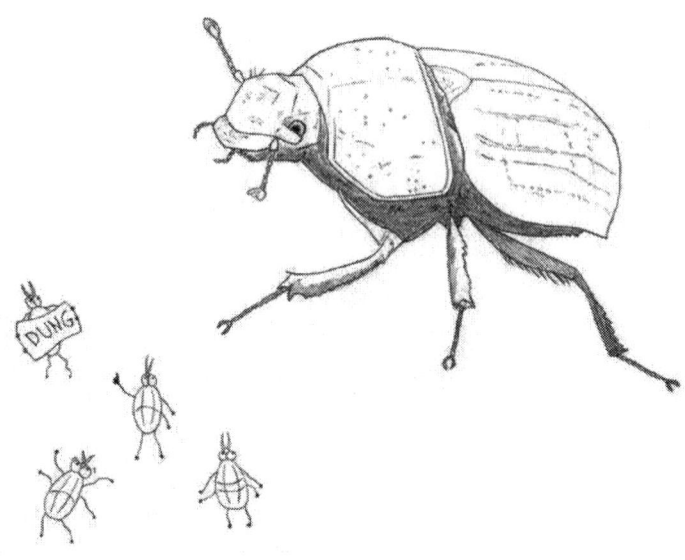

"Dung! Dung! Du –"

"QUIET!"

Silence followed.

"Excitable bunch – don't even eat the D-word, per se – little blighters gobble up mould growing in the dung. Can you imagine that? Leaving the best bits to waste!"

"Do they … hurt?"

"Hurt? Nonsense! Little devils just hitch a ride – and, by eating mould in the dung I leave for my larvae, they keep my nippers' meals fresh – as if straight from the cow! Grown quite fond of them actually, my phoretic friends…"

"Dung! Dung! Dung!"

"Doesn't that get annoying?"

"Nonsense … well, yes, actually, incredibly annoying … but it's certainly better than what they used to chant. Such obscenities! Got to rule with a firm tarsus, that's what I say. Now, how may I be of service?"

"I'm looking for the tundra."

"Tundra? Never heard of one. What's it eat?"

"Err ... it's more of a place than a creature. It freezes in winter ... at least I think it does."

"Freezes! Can't be doing with that. Frozen dung's no good for eating..." Mr Dor poked at the ground with one leg, just to check it hadn't iced over. "Now then ... where were we?"

"Dung! Dung! Dung!"

"Ah yes, we need to traverse that mountainous peak," He lumbered towards a small pebble beside my feet. "Now, let's see ... legs up, one, two..." he started to climb, "Oh dear," and tipped onto his back, revealing glossy purple undersides dotted with brown mites.

I lowered my beak to his level. "Can I help?"

"Nonsense … well, probably … but I'm a professional, I'll be fine. I've got a plan. Let's get legs one and two flailing … now legs three and four … and then supported by a little flailing from legs five and six…" Mr Dor rocked on his carapace, front legs reaching out, hooking onto a grass stem – he started to turn himself over … but the grass slipped away, "Curses!" he said, now spinning *and* rocking on his back. "Thought we'd had it then."

"Are you sure I can't…"

"Won't hear of it. Professional integrity. Now, about your tundra, it can't have gone far. Best ask the Bumblebees – delightful young ladies – very knowledgeable too. Now then … where were we?"

"Dung! Dung! Du –"

"Quiet! Hush now. I've got a plan for righting us. It involves a bit of flailing, but I think it might just work…"

I left him rocking back and forth, legs flailing to the chant of *"Dung! Dung! Dung!"*

And that was the day I went in search of Bumblebees.

Mites!

Never travel by unlicensed Dor Beetle!

EIGHT

Finding Bumblebees was easy. Talking to them was tricky.

Buzz Buzz Buzz – that's all I got for days on end. Buzz Buzz Buzz – as they zipped and zoomed from flower to flower – black and yellow streaks. Eventually, as the days grew longer and hotter, there seemed to be more of them about, and I got a brisk, "Buzz Buzz *Busy* – can't stop..." And that was that.

But on a cold drizzly day – slap bang in the middle of summer – I caught up with one. In fact, I nearly trod on the thing as it sheltered in a flower, all sad and bedraggled, fur beaded with water. Sorry looking critter.

"Excuse me, Miss..."

"Stay back, foul creature..." she waved her middle legs in the air, "...or feel my wrath."

"Okay…" I stayed back, "Let's not overreact…"

"Don't EVER tell me how to act, Goose … or I will make your blood boil…"

"Right…" just for once, it would've been nice for everything to go smoothly – no death threats, no lies, no confusion – just a simple *'Hi there, which way to the tundra? That way? Thank you so much! Goodbye.'* I'd had enough … so I didn't stay back, I stepped forward, towards the furious furry little ball, "I don't mean to be … *mean* … but I could tread on you – squish you with one webbed foot – *but I won't,*" I added, "because I'm a bigger goose than that."

"You dare think yourself capable of crushing me? Tell me, *foul bird* … did your parents not speak to you about the birds and the bees?"

"Err … I think I missed out on that story, before…" *A tall white stalk, slicing petals, feathers splayed across the sky,* "…before." I finished, swiping the memories aside.

"Then let me tell you how the story ends: the birds ALWAYS LOSE." She brandished the black point of her sting. "Now let us re-enact the fable…"

"Don't you die if you sting me?"

"Ha! The ignorance! That is a cruel lie, no doubt spread by my male brethren, whose own sting is conspicuous by its absence. A cruel lie indeed – but only to those who believe it. Observe…" Fully unsheathed, the sting was a sharp, black talon, "my spine is smooth … I can strike repeatedly with no impairment to myself – now be gone – for *my* sting strikes true…"

"Steady, Miss…" I took a step back from the vibrating fuzzball, "Maybe if you tell me what I've done wrong, I could say sorry – and you could not sting me – and I could find my flock and have a happy ending. What do you say, Miss?"

"Ha! That is your crime, Goose. I am not to be addressed as 'Miss' – I am a 'Ms'."

"Miz?"

"*Ms*." Her wings quivered, "Not 'Mrs', not 'Miss'... I am a *Ms* – Mzzzzz. All day long I have to assert my right to anonymity. Always travelling to and fro: Mzzzzz between flowers, Mzzzzz to the birds, Mzzzzz to that infernal Dor Beetle. Mzzzzz. Mzzzzz. Mzzzzzzzzzzzzz. Do you understand, goose? Does your pea-sized brain grasp the concept?"

I looked at her tiny head. "How small do peas go?"

"What was that?!"

"Err … I said, *'I'll have another go'* – at addressing you, Ms, now that I understand…"

"You do not understand!"

"Nope, you're right, you saw through me on that one. Maybe you could explain, Mz…"

The 'Mz' calmed her down. The sting was once again sheathed in the fur of her abdomen.

"Listen carefully," she said, "The term 'Miss' refers to worker bees. 'Mrs' refers to queens. The term 'Ms' does not distinguish between the two – preserving my right to anonymity."

"Anno what now?"

"My right to conceal my role within the colony."

"I see." I didn't. "So will you be a queen one day – a *Mrs* Bumblebee?"

"Ha! The life of romance and egg laying is not for the worker bee. Our roles are fixed at brood rearing. Ha! If my sisters could hear you – become a queen! Only those reared on a banquet of food become queens – and only if her current Majesty permits it, through pheromone control."

"So ... what you're saying is ... you're always going to be a worker – a 'Miss'"

"Toiling for the good of the colony, yes." Her wings stopped quivering.

"And there's no chance of you becoming queen – a 'Mrs'?"

"Correct." She folded her wings neatly over her back.

"And does anyone else in the colony know this?"

"Yes. Every member: all one hundred and twelve of them."

"But…" the world felt like it was spinning, "you still want to be referred to as 'Ms', to hide what everyone already knows?"

"Correct – preserving my *right* to anonymity, if not *actual* anonymity itself."

"Okay … I think I'm beginning to see…" *Double* – I was beginning to see double – and strange lights – and the inside of my head – and a tiny grain of pollen floating on the wind – and all the other bizarre things you notice when your brain stalls."

"Well," I said, "that's all very clear. As clear as … a very clear thing."

"Then our discussion has been a success. If only all ignorant creatures were as adept at learning the blindingly obvious – then I wouldn't have to constantly remind them I'm a Mzzzzz. Good day to you, goose."

"Goodbye Miss … I mean…"

"Mzzzzzzzzzzzzzzzzzzzzzzzzzzzzzzzzzzzzzzzzzzzzzzzzzzz
zzzzzzzzzzzzzzzzzzzzzzzzzzzzzzzzzzzzzzzzzzzzz."

By the time her *Mzzing* died away, I realised I hadn't actually asked her for directions, so I continued to head for the hills.

And that was the day when I started to lose hope.

NINE

Paddling upriver was hard – but paddling upstream? That was *rock* hard – literally – mostly due to the large amount of rocks. In fact, there were more rocks to scramble over than water to swim in – and that small amount of water was feisty – steep and fast and rushing against me. If I'd stopped paddling – even for a moment – I would've been spat off the hillside.

So I got out and walked. The rolling hills were endless as I flopped and slumped over the springy purple heather. It was all hot sun, treeless slopes, and ... *things*.

Things lurked in the heather. I could see black beady eyes, framed by red, chuckling at me: an empty hill of chuckling eyes. My *mouse pimples* returned in force.

"Go back!" croaked a clump of heather, and I stumbled, tripped and rolled. "Go back!" A head poked out of the clump – then the rest of the creature – a squat, chestnut-coloured bird, huge red wattles arched over its beady eyes.

"Who are you?" I held out my wings to balance on the bouncing heather.

"We are Grouse," said the bird, "Now ... go back, go back, GO BACK!"

"Can't." I held my beak high, "I have to keep going – to find my flock. I've overcome Bumblebees and Bullfinches to get here ... you can't stop me."

"Ha, ha, hah," chuckled the Grouse, "Not us – it's the NUBs – with their shiny branches that spit fire and smoke and make you go POOF! An explosion of feathers."

"The NUBs are here? Now? On this hill?"

"Oh yes, it's all kicking off soon. *They're* raring to go; *we're* raring to go. If we were any rarer, we'd all be Dotterel."

"What do you mean by 'kicking off'?"

"Ha, ha, hah," said the Grouse, "Soon the beating of the heather begins, signalling the start of the games: the NUBs line up, shiny branches poised, ready to do their species proud. The Wheatear tells me last year's efforts were truly inspirational – a pile of dead grouse – the streams ran red with blood – we only hope we can surpass those efforts..."

"You only hope?!! You want this to happen?"

"Of course. It's the order of things. Ever since ... The Twelfth."

"The what?"

"The Twelfth – surely you've heard of The Twelfth – he was a famous grouse ... *The* famous grouse. Long ago, when the NUBs first arrived, he was the twelfth grouse to be killed – but the first to realise the danger – the first to give warning to his fellow grouse. 'Go Back!' he croaked, 'Go Back!' before being cut down in an explosion of feathers – glorious he was – The Glorious Twelfth!" The Grouse swelled significantly with pride, "So now we all shout, 'Go back,' to honour him, his sacrifice, his intelligence, and ensure no other grouse need meet the same fate."

"Does it work?"

"Ha, ha, hah," laughed the Grouse, "not even slightly ... because once the NUBs begin ... well, no grouse can resist taking flight. It's the excitement ... the anticipation ... the only sound is the beating of heather – beating in time with our hearts ... the surge of adrenaline as we take flight ... the uncertainty – not knowing what's to come – what's waiting for us on the ridge – but at the same time knowing that only *we* can influence the result – only *we* can determine a flight or a fall. We say, *'Go Back'*, but there's no going back, there's only forwards and up ... or forwards and down." He leaned in, red wattles raised, "You never feel more alive ... than when you have power over death."

"Err ... I see." I didn't (again), "Couldn't you try stay put ... or sneak around the NUBs?"

"Ha, ha, hah – of course – but where's the fun in that? Where's the *showgrouseship*?"

"Then why bother shouting, 'Go Back'?"

"Tradition. We can't abandon tradition – where would we be without it?"

"Alive?"

"Ha, ha, hah – a cynic – but just you watch: we're about to have another go…" He pointed his beak towards a distant clump of heather: a plump grouse shot up into the air, soared briefly, and then frantically beat its wings.

"Go back…" croaked the Grouse beside me, "Go back, go back, go back…" **BANG, POOF!** An explosion of feathers. The distant grouse dropped to the floor, no longer flapping. The Grouse beside me gave a throaty chuckle, "Ha, ha, hah … I told him, I said *'go back, go back, go back.'* Good try though, entering the spirit of things … and he almost made it. Ha, ha, hah, gotta laugh, gotta have a sense of humour." And then the heather exploded. "CHEEKY!" roared the Grouse, "False start!" Another cackle – like thunder – and the pine sapling beside me disintegrated. "Ha, ha, hah, carrying on regardless, good sport!" the Grouse turned to me, "Looks like we're up next: may the best bird win…" and, with a slapping flap, he shot out of the heather and into the air, "Ha, ha, hah … the thrill of it – just FEEL the thrill of it…" he surged over the hills, "Ha, ha, hah – oh wait…" he was somehow flying without flapping ... and without most of his feathers ... and in a fairly downwards direction as the hillside echoed with thunder. "They got me! Blast," said the Grouse, "pun intended," and dropped to ground, dead.

I hunkered down. There was a smell in the air – the smell of me, after I'd fallen from the sky that first time – a bit like smoke from a forest fire. There were no bird calls – not so much as a pipit. I thought maybe the NUBs had gone ... until the heather erupted in a shower of scorched sprigs.

I scrambled up and over the clumps, not looking back ... and the hill ended. I fell towards rushing water. CRASH – straight into the moorland stream, batted from rock to rock, frantically paddling to avoid being skewered on sharp edges. Thunder boomed everywhere – I couldn't tell if it was the NUBs, my own impact against the rocks, or a real storm.

Onwards and downwards I paddled ... the rocks became fewer, the stream became wider ... but I didn't look back. The sun set and rose again – I don't know how many times – before I dared dabble for some slimy weed in the river. But I didn't look back. A cool breeze, growing cooler with each day, ruffled my feathers and blew me faster downriver. The weed did nothing for my appetite and the last of my energy drained away. I floated in a cold, numb silence ... but I didn't look back.

Finally, exhausted and starving, I dared to glance upriver: the big hills of the Grouse looked very small. My chance of reaching a vantage point was lost. I could be on *any* river, maybe even floating south, away from the tundra ... but I didn't have the energy to care.

And that was the day I tucked my beak under my wing ... for what I thought would be the last time.

TEN

Peck peck peck ... and then nothing. *Peck peck peck peck peck...* Something – or more accurately, *lots of somethings* – pecked quietly away at my feathers with their tiny beaks. This was good, because it meant I was alive, but also bad, because it meant I was being pecked.

I lifted my head out from under my wing, readying myself (as much as a terminally exhausted goose can) to fight off the swarm of attackers. I looked around and saw ... nothing. Nothing but reeds and – *OUCH!* Something jabbed me in the eye.

"Where are you?" I span around – *OUCH!* It hit me a second time.

"Show yourself! Bring it on!" *OUCH!*

And then it did show itself ... it showed itself to be a huge monster leering over me with twisted limbs – it was a Larch tree.

OUCH! Another of its falling needles hit me in the eye.

Wind rattled the branches and I *goosed* underwater to avoid being peppered by debris. With the barrage over, I swam to the bank, stepped out, and waddled to shelter under a Pine tree. Pine trees were reliable – they didn't go in for all this 'moulting at the slightest drop in temperature'. If only they'd grown something edible.

Food... I was just wondering where I could get a decent meal, when the undergrowth exploded with a shriek:

"Keeyarrrrh!"

A Buzzard! *Where is it?* I tripped over a fallen pinecone, honked in panic, and looked for a silhouette in the sky.

Should I goose-and-cover, or waddle for it? A Juniper bush sat close by. *I can make that. Probably.*

"Keeyarrrrh!" So close – it was *everywhere* – but there was no sign, no silhouette. Uncle Joe's words shot through my head:

"What do I say about Buzzards ... that you hear a whoosh of air ... then you're dead."

Whoosh of air! That wasn't very helpful when you lived in the windiest land of all...

"**Keeyarrrh!**" *So close ... almost on me ... here we go...*

I heard a whoosh of air ... Larch needles scattered on the breeze ... and then a Buzzard stepped out of the Juniper bush.

"**Kee**–" but the second part of its call fell into a hacking "ack ack ack," as the chunky bird of prey coughed, "Terribly sorry," said the Buzzard, "bit of a frog in my throat." It coughed again and something slimy shot out of its beak and splatted on the ground: it was the leg of an amphibian.

"Much better," said the Buzzard, and peered down at the slimy leg, "Well I'll be damned – a toad! Fancy that." The bird straightened up. I watched the ripple of every feather, the glint of each talon, the sharp hook of its beak – and waited for the end. I continued to wait while the Buzzard shifted from one foot to the other, "I was wondering..." it eventually began, "...if you might permit me the honour of asking a favour of you?"

The words rattled around my head for a long time before I understood them.

"*You* ... want to ask *me* ... a favour?" It was some sort of trick – it had to be – and I knew the finale would involve talons in my gizzard.

"Yes please," said the Buzzard, "You see ... I'm in a spot of bother. Had a run in with one of those mineral shells in which the NUBs are always gallivanting around. One clip of the old wings and that's *Yours Truly* grounded. Now I must say ... I do *like* seeing the NUBs around – I'm pro-mammal, don't get me wrong – but I feel maybe there's a tad too many of them. Do we really need all of those NUBs? What do they do? Imagine the effect they're having on the small mammal population – don't see so many Water Voles these days, do you? A coincidence? I think not!"

In my peripheral vision, I could just see the reeds: the edge of the river and freedom.

Stalling time... "About this favour?"

"Ah yes, I do apologise." He flexed his talons. "Well ... suffice to say, since I've been grounded, I've been dining on worms and the odd amphibian – nothing wrong with that, mind you. Mummy always said, 'a meal on the ground is not one to ever turn down'. Never quite mastered the art of rhyme, bless her. Anyhow, long story short, eating all this wriggly sliminess gives me a dickie tummy. So I was wondering if – and this is where it gets quite awkward, really – I was wondering if I could ... eat you."

"Eat me?"

"Well ... yes, if it's not too much of an inconvenience. I'd be awfully grateful." He leaned forwards, expectantly.

"Errrrrrrrr," my longest one yet, "I'd rather you didn't?" I felt I was trying to guess the answer to a deadly riddle.

"Of course, of course." The Buzzard straightened up. "Entirely your decision – and I respect it wholeheartedly."

"You do?"

"Absolutely. A raptor's word is his bond. But tell me – did I come across as too brash? Too forward? Haven't had much luck, you see, with the other forest creatures ... although a squirrel considered it at length. I don't mind admitting ... I'm so terribly hungry."

"Too brash," I said, gaze fixed on that sharp beak, "that's exactly it."

"Ah ... suspected as much. Not normally much time for a *tête-à-tête* in the due course of things – the odd 'Keeyarrrrh' here and there, as the mood takes one – and then it's mostly grabbing, ripping and spilled innards. Suppose I've lost touch with the common bird on the ground."

"So..." I wanted to be really sure, "...you're not going to eat me?"

"'Fraid not, old Bean Goose, but *c'est la vie*. Must say though … you are looking a trifle stringy."

"I've been … travelling." *He doesn't know I can't fly – that might just be keeping me alive.* "Well…" I took a step back, "I should be going now…"

"Best of luck, *bon voyage* and all that…"

There was a moment of silence in which we stared at each other. There was no way I would turn my back on him – but at the same time, edging away seemed a bit rude.

"If you don't mind," I said, "I'm going to back away now. No offence."

"Of course," said the Buzzard, "Very wise, very prudent – don't know who you can trust these days. *Au revoir, mon ami…*"

"Bye…" I stepped back through the reeds and into the river, not quite knowing if I'd outwitted a slippery genius, or simply a very odd bird.

Paddling downriver, the channel widened, becoming calm. I don't know for how many sunrises and sunsets I drifted. The hills slowly browned, the Alders lost all their leaves, the wind became freezing, and one day … I'd had enough. As the sun sank below the now-distant hills, the sky glowed orange and then red. Finally, as purple darkness descended, I tucked my head under my wing and let the current take me.

And that was the day I drifted out to sea.

ELEVEN

In the darkness, I heard honking ... and then: Slam – a wave, ice cold, smashed over me ... and then another: Slam, SLAM, SLAM! Except this wasn't fear – this was outside me – wet, cold, salty.

I unfolded my head and neck and peered out at the grey sea on which I bobbed. SLAM! Another pesky wave broke over my head. And in the distance, I heard honking – real geese, not in my mind. The gentle honking of White-fronts.

But from where? From everywhere, that was the answer. No help whatsoever. The honking could've come from any one of the rocky islands scattered along the coast.

I'll check them, I'll check them all until ... what was that?

A tiny grey fin rolled up out of the waves and then vanished.

"Hello?" I called, "Anyone there?"

The fin appeared again, turning on a tight ball of grey – a body? – and a voice said:

"Please be quiet, please be silent. Don't tell –" and the fin plunged back under the waves.

"I'm sorry, I didn't catch that."

The fin emerged again:

"…anyone I'm here, especially not –" the voice cut off as the fin sliced back down into the water.

I bobbed once, twice, then the fin reappeared:

"…the Dolphins. They'll beat me, they'll bash me, and –"

Gone. I looked around. Uncle Joe had mentioned Dolphins – mammals disguised as giant cackling fish. Shockingly, he didn't trust them.

Up popped the fin:

"...and hit me and hurt me and –"

"NO DOLPHINS HERE!" I honked.

"Oh." The fin stopped in mid rotation. A blunt, grey creature floated to the surface and peered at me through tiny black eyes. "Oh," it said, "that's good, that's very good, but I can't stay, they could be here any minute…"

"Who are you?"

"I'm Porpoise…" it swam in nervous circles.

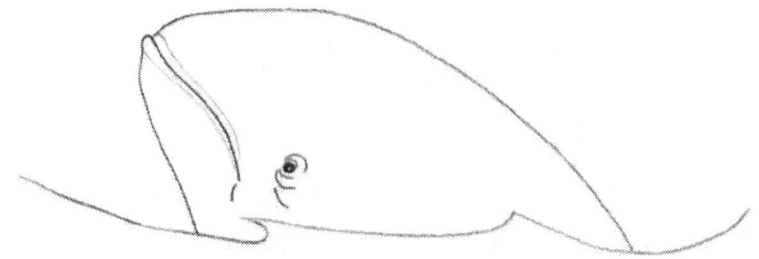

"Why are the Dolphins after you?"

"To beat me, for fun, for practice. I have to go, have to swim, can't stop, can't ever stop…" the fin started to rotate.

"Wait! Please … can you tell me where that honking's coming from? Where are the geese? The geese like me?"

"They were on the second island out from the mainland – I'd take you there, but it's where THEY lurk, always waiting, watching, ready to pounce and bite and … oh dear!" the fin rolled back into the water and, with a delicate little splash, the creature vanished.

I was left bobbing, occasionally slapped by impatient waves.

Right: second island out from the mainland. One, two – easy. I could deal with one and two – any higher and things become a little fuzzy. *One, two – here goes…*

Blasted by salt, I thrashed my way up the towering waves, plunged into deep troughs, closer and closer to that second island – little more than a grey blob. But the blob grew, flattening out, spreading across the horizon. I could see woodland, beaches, mudflats ... and there, above a patch of marsh, coming into roost, not quite darkening the sky, were geese – brown, honking geese. Their white patches blazed in the sun.

And that was the day, after an entire season alone, that I found my flock.

TWELVE

They were all there – Mr and Mrs White, *Mr and Mrs Front*, White Senior, *Old Whitey*, Old Whitey Junior, *Junior Whitey*, Madame Front, *Whiteness Esquire (The Third)*... and they all looked a bit ... samey.

It didn't take long to find Uncle Joe.

"Whitey?! You're alive! It's a miracle. We'd given up hope. What did I say about his chances of survival?" He looked around for someone to complete his sentence – someone who Uncle Joe would then enjoy interrupting to complete the sentence himself. But no other geese came forward, so Uncle Joe had to do everything: "...I said: his chance of survival is zero."

But you were wrong, I wanted to honk, loudly, but instead, I asked, "What did you get up to?"

"Get up to?" Uncle Joe fixed me with a stare, "Get up to?! What do you think we got up to? Eat, breed, lay, hatch, rear, fledge, fly. The circle of life."

Seems more like a line to me.

"But..." I clung onto my politeness, "...don't you have any interesting stories to tell?"

"Stories ... stories ... well, I fledged four goslings this year, Mr and Mrs White fledged three..."

"But what about other creatures? How are the Pink-feet doing? The wild Greylags? Do they have Bumblebees in the tundra yet?"

"Bumble ... *bees*?"

"Yes. You know – furry little critters – buzzing and angry."

He gave a shrug of his wings.

"Well ... didn't you meet anyone?"

"Meet? Meet?! No time for meeting. It's all eat, breed, lay, hatch, rear, fledge, fly ... and then eat again, if there's time."

"Then what about the journey back?"

"Eat, roost, fly..."

"But..." and I was now clutching at reeds, "...didn't you talk to *any* other creature? Didn't you even see a Porpoise?"

"Don't speak to me in that hoity-toity tone – of course I saw a purpose – the purpose was to eat, breed, lay, hatch –"

"No. Not purpose – *Porpoise*."

"Purpose, porpoise ... don't try to be smart with me. Listen, Whitey, you need to get your birdbrain in order – all this time alone has sent you funny. All this talk of ... well ... of talking – it's not right. What did I say the isolation would do to his sanity?" Another glance around, but still no goose paddled up to the mark, "I said: the isolation will send him –"

"Uncle Joe…" My interruption shut him up. He wasn't used to interruptions. "I just wanted to mention, that everything you say – *and I do mean everything* – is a load of Bullfinch."

And in that moment, I thought back on every creature from my journey: heartbroken Snipe, brave Lapwings, worried Greylag, tireless Mr Dor, agitated Ms Bumblebee, glory-seeking Grouse, and petrified Porpoise. If I'd migrated, I would have missed out on each encounter. And it'd been fun (mostly) – even with Bullfinch – it'd been fun picking apart his lies. *Even* with the Buzzard – mind you, that had been scary fun – *guano scary* fun – but thrilling – and so much more than *eat, breed, lay, hatch, rear, fledge, fly,* repeat, forever. *One day … maybe. But not today. No thank you.*

So I said, "I'm leaving the flock."

"Leaving the flock?" This jolted Uncle Joe to life. The flock could leave behind a goose – no problem – but for a goose to leave behind the flock – that was heresy. "Leaving the flock?! Let me tell you, Whitey: you've already left – in your head – you left it a long time ago, just like your parents. They were dreamers, drifters – and what did I say would happen?" There was no glance around this time, "I said: they'll end up –"

"Uncle Joe," I spoke quietly, but firmly, "Don't. Don't ever speak about my parents like that again..." I channelled the threatening malice of a crow, "...if you know what's good for you."

In the silence that followed, I turned and paddled away. Maybe I'd go see if Mr Dor had righted himself by now, maybe I'd try guide Porpoise to a safe haven, or maybe I'd go see what actually lay on the other side of the hills – rather than Bullfinch's imaginary purple ocean. Maybe I'd do all of those things ... but first, I glanced back at Uncle Joe:

"And another thing..." I said, before swimming away, "...what kind of a stupid name for a goose is Joe?"

And that, my friends, was the day I started my life...

Additional stories by P. J. Taylor

Waiting

A young woman waits in hospital. She's alone, having driven all her friends away out of jealousy and fear. As for her dad, he'd rather bury his head in a textbook than talk to his daughter about life and death – because it's crunch time: if her operation doesn't go well, that's it, her cancer will have won.

There isn't much time left to fix her relationships, but when you're waiting, time seems to last just that little bit longer.

'Waiting' is a short story suitable for young and not-so-young adults. An ideal read for a brief train journey, passing time until the next bus, or any other circumstances in which you find yourself waiting…

Available on Amazon Kindle.

Additional stories by P. J. Taylor

The Third Party

Scotland: the near future.

Could wolves be reintroduced to the Highlands?

A tired politician listens as the debate rages. Representatives for and against the venture are full of passion, conflicting facts, and entrenched stubbornness.

Yet, unknown to both sides, someone else is working silently on their own, very different, agenda: the third party.

A short story suitable for adult and young adult readers.

Available as a free pdf download from www.blackerminetales.co.uk

Click on the 'FREEBIES' tab.

Printed in Great Britain
by Amazon.co.uk, Ltd.,
Marston Gate.